Credos
& Quips

By Virginia Cary Hudson

O Ye Jigs & Juleps!
Credos & Quips

Credos
&
Quips

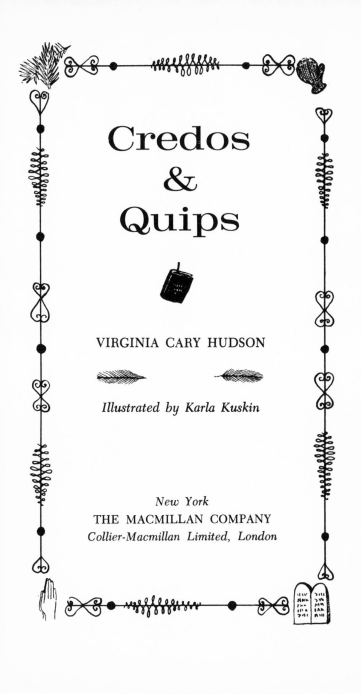

VIRGINIA CARY HUDSON

Illustrated by Karla Kuskin

New York
THE MACMILLAN COMPANY
Collier-Macmillan Limited, London

Text copyright © Virginia Cleveland Mayne 1964

Illustrations copyright © Karla Kuskin 1964

Third Printing 1964

The Macmillan Company, New York
Collier-Macmillan Canada Ltd., Toronto, Ontario

Library of Congress catalog card number: 64-22161

Printed in the United States of America

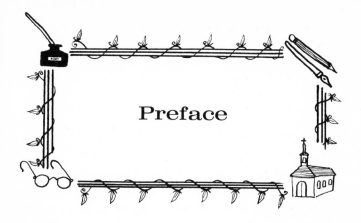

Preface

In 1954, at the age of fifty-nine, my mother, Virginia Hudson Cleveland, died while talking to one of her dearest friends. All her life she loved to talk and to put down on paper the things that she talked about. From the age of ten, when she wrote the fresh and uninhibited school compositions that were published a few years ago as *O Ye Jigs & Juleps!* through the years during which she confined her sharp and perceptive observations of human behavior to family letters, and to the completion of the following essays, she loved always to tell others what she thought about the world, religion, and human behavior.

These four essays, then, are a kind of compendium of my mother's belief and how she felt about it. She was not the kind that kept things to herself. When she believed something, she wanted others to know that she believed it, and why. This is the reason she wrote down these statements of what she believed and why she gave them as talks to her Guild at Calvary Episcopal Church in Louisville, Kentucky.

My mother was not a theologian; neither was she a historian. What she says in these little talks, therefore, is not to be taken as a pure theological statement of Episcopalian belief or as a scholar's factual presentation of history. What she has done is to put forth for the average churchgoer a rich and earnest devotional plea enlivened by her own particular brand of humor. Some of her humor is earthy; she did not live on a rarefied plane. She knew the foibles and failings of human beings and she never hesitated to point them out in the bluntest terms. On the other hand, she possessed a rare gift of linking human failings with spiritual aspirations; this was one of her greatest gifts.

The reader who is looking for a catechism or for a history of religious thought is well advised to seek other sources of information. My mother did not write to inform. She wrote to bring others to that flame by which she warmed herself and others close to her. As with all of us, separated by a number of years from our early religious teaching, facts sometimes blend into legend; details are obscured, and one's own personal discoveries loom largest in the religious vision that illuminates one's own life. So it was with Virginia. She longed to show others her personal vision; her means of doing it was through humor and hardheaded sense. That she was successful is amply testified to us by the following memorial that appeared in her parish bulletin at the time of her death:

"Her education, acquired, as it were, under the eaves of the Church, endowed her with a fund of unique and rarely found knowledge of many things pertaining to the Church. The imparting of this knowledge was always embellished with curious and humorous anecdotes which always made her frequent 'talks' and readings most interesting and unforgettable. Her personal attraction, together with her devotion to Calvary, will long remain embedded upon the tablets of our minds and hearts."

Unforgettable she was—to her friends, to her family, and to the many thousands who read *O Ye Jigs & Juleps!* To these this new book of the writings of Virginia grown up is presented with the hope that it will give them as much joy as her early work, and a new perspective on the many sides of Virginia Cary Hudson.

VIRGINIA C. MAYNE

Contents

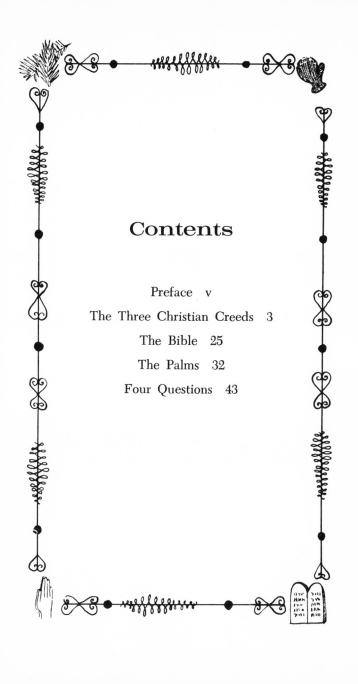

Credos
& Quips

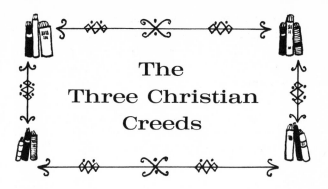

The Three Christian Creeds

No man has ever "to get religion." He already has it. He is born with a realization of a Superior and Supreme Being, which is all that religion is. The experience he undergoes which he thinks is "getting religion" is only an awakened concept of what is already there, awaiting his grasp and use of it. We nurse, with our mother's milk, the type of faith we generally retain throughout our lives. When we convert our feeling to another type of faith, we do not "change our religion," because it is unchangeable. We, ourselves, merely change over to another form of expression of the same principle, more in keeping with our own individual reasoning and personal need. All conviction generates an assertion, and if that assertion is sincere, it will be followed by manifestation. We assert with words. We manifest with deeds and the false coupling of one with the other constitutes hypocrisy.

3

The assertions of the Christian faith are its creeds, and Christians are the supposed followers of a Galilean named Jesu Christus. Many of them select from His teachings those which serve their own purpose and convenience. His teachings which do not comply with their motives, they evade by verbal acrobatics, making it appear, to their own satisfaction, that He did not mean it exactly that way. Heaven is such a charming place. All of us are just going to love Heaven. But Hell—don't mention Hell, if you please, not to the intelligentsia. To them Hell is primitive and utterly naïve. This hocus-pocus selective salve, spread on the evasive hides of Christians, and self-applied, is the balm of the Devil and is anti-Christ: contrary to His very words.

The Catholic churches comprise one-half of all the earth's population; the Protestant movement contains one-third. We Christians, who say that ours is the only faith, have always had in our own ranks more dissension than has existed in any other religious belief. Two thousand years is ample time for the world to have become Christian, if we had joined ranks in pure purpose of the practice of that which we profess.

There are three creeds in the Christian churches, the word *credo* meaning "I believe." They are the Apostles' Creed, the Nicene Creed, and the Athanasian Creed. These creeds which are a confession of faith, should not be looked upon as representing men's thinking, or a system of speculative opinion;

4

but rather as an epitome of recorded and established fact, measuring up to a specified rule of belief.

The historical evidence is now missing, but the earliest Christian tradition asserts and maintains that the Apostles met in Jerusalem, and each one of them contributed an article of belief to form an authentic, compendious and unchangeable declaration of inspired knowledge. The following twelve articles forming the original Apostles' Creed are thus; the words in parentheses having been added in the year 650 at Ephesus:

1—I believe in God the Father (maker of heaven and earth)
2—And in Jesus Christ His only Son our Lord.
3—Who was conceived by the Holy Ghost, born of the Virgin Mary
4—Suffered under Pontius Pilate, was crucified and buried. (dead) (He descended into Hell)
5—The third day He rose again from the dead.
6—He ascended into Heaven
7—And sitteth on the right hand of the Father. (God) (Almighty)
8—From thence He shall come to judge the quick and the dead.
9—I believe in the Holy Ghost
10—The Holy Church (Catholic)
11—The resurrection of the body
12—The forgiveness of sins. Amen (and life Everlasting)

5

The nucleus of the Creed, Father, Son, and Holy Ghost, has been adopted as the formula of Baptism.

The Nicene Creed, contrary to popular belief, was not written at Nice, but was drawn up at Constantinople in 381, and is an amplification of the original started at Nice nearly sixty years previously.

This 381 creed reads thus: "I believe in one God the Father Almighty, maker of heaven and earth, and of all things visible and invisible; and in one Lord Jesus Christ, the only begotten Son of God, Begotten of his Father before all worlds, God of God, Light of Light, Very God of Very God; Begotten, not made, Being of one Substance with the Father; By whom all things were made: who for us men and our salvation came down from heaven, and was incarnate by the Holy Ghost of the Virgin Mary, and was made man: and was crucified also for us under Pontius Pilate: He suffered and was buried: And the third day he rose again according to the Scriptures: And ascended into heaven, and sitting on the right hand of the Father; and He shall come again, with glory, to judge both the quick and the dead; Whose kingdom shall have no end.

"And I believe in the Holy Ghost, the Lord, and Giver of Life, who proceedeth from the Father and the Son: who with the Father and the Son is worshipped and glorified: Who spoke by the Prophets: and I believe in one Catholic and Apostolic church. I acknowledge one Baptism for the remission of sins: And I look for the Resurrection of the

dead: and the life of the world to come. Amen."
That "one" Baptism does not mean one mode of
baptism, but does mean rather to be Baptized only
once, or one time.

The enlargement of the Apostles' Creed, evolving
in the Nicene Creed, began at Nice in 325, as also
did the birth-pangs of the Athanasian Creed. There,
the men of God met to have it out concerning the
Trinity and there were 318 bishops in the front
ring-side boxes. If you think that the truce talks have
taken up too much time, or that the United Nations
sessions will never end, you should study the de-
bates of the Christians. For fifty-six years they kept
up one argument—at Nice, and at Nice again; at
Antioch in 341; at Sardica in 347; at Arles in 353;
at Milan in 355, and the final bell and last round,
at Constantinople in 381. These ecclesiastical oral
pugilists tightened their personal girth, and lacing
their religious gloves, they hit below the belt, vio-
lating every code of the Christ in whose name they
fought. Heresy was not enough. They accused one
another of rape, of the practice of magical arts, and
they even resorted to the employment of poison to
remove their opponents. They disrobed, and condemned, and banished one another. The opposing
forces were led by Arius and Athanasius, and not
until Arius doubled up on the street and died, with
belly-cramps from poison, did the fight subside.
Arius was only a priest of Alexandria but Athanasius was his Bishop, and this Bishop standing in
the conference, dedicated to Christ, clenched his
fist, and beat upon his breast, and roared out to

God to remove Arius. History insinuates that it was Athanasius, and not God, who removed Arius.

The views of Arius did not die with him. As late as the sixteenth century we find the English church issuing an order "that the incorrigible Arians be sent to a castle in North Wales, to live by their own labor and none to resort to them save their keepers." Arius imbibed his idea of Jesus from a Greek of Antioch named Lucian, who conducted the first Christian theological school ever in session, and who was taken in chains to Nicomedia and tortured to death. It has been over forty years since I studied the doctrines of Arius and Athanasius, and this is what they meant to me. The Christ of Athanasius was identical with God in Power and Being, all God. The Christ of Arius was a separate Sonship derived from and begotten. Hence apart from God, since even God could not beget Himself. Separate from God in scriptural soundness. Christ is to sit on God's right hand. God does not sit on his own right hand. Christ prayed to, and besought, God. No God prays to Himself. Proof of separate Godheads, "Thy will be done, not mine" and "My God, why hast Thou forsaken me?" To Arius God was not begotten, never conceived, cannot be born, nor can He die. All four circumstances were true of Jesus. The Christ of Arius was the Son of God, with accent on the Son, and the Saviour of all men. At every sentence of Arius, Athanasius would scream out, "Blasphemy." Such ravings would have distracted the attention, and confused the speech of a man weaker in conviction than was Arius. Nothing halted him. Only death stopped him. He

8

was a bold thinker, and an eloquent and persuasive disciple of argument. Had he outlived the scheming Athanasius, it is very likely that we might think differently today. Arius was a firebrand of zeal, igniting men's personal reasoning, based on the infallibility of the Scriptures, rather than condoning a set form of orthodox opinion construed by another.

At the time of Arius' death, his sympathizers were gaining in number and strength. For a period of four months prior to this time, Athanasius had been forced to hide in his father's tomb, and it was during a six-year sentence of exile that he wrote the creed which bears his name. It has been thought, and proposed that this creed bears the name of Athanasius, because it voices his contention, rather than having been written by him himself. Since this creed was written in his lifetime I cannot think that he did not write it. He of all people, of his generation, needed no man to frame his words. He was the all-time high of all exegetes, and with Arius gone, he became a flesh and blood dynamo, supplying magnetizing theological current to the early church.

The following is the Bute translation, or the English translation of the Athanasian Creed:

Whosoever will be saved, before all things it is necessary that he hold the Catholic Faith, which Faith except everyone do keep whole and undefiled, without doubt he shall perish everlastingly. And the Catholic Faith is this, that we worship one God in Trinity and Trinity in Unity. Neither

10

confounding the Persons, nor dividing the Substance. For there is one Person of the Father, another of the Son, and another of the Holy Ghost. But the Godhead of the Father, and of the Son, and of the Holy Ghost is all One, the Glory Equal, the Majesty Co-Eternal. Such as the Father is, such is the Son, and such is the Holy Ghost. The Father uncreate, the Son uncreate, and the Holy Ghost uncreate. The Father Incomprehensible, the Son Incomprehensible, and the Holy Ghost Incomprehensible. The Father Eternal, the Son Eternal, and the Holy Ghost Eternal, and yet they are not Three Eternals, but One Eternal, as also there are not Three Eternals but One Eternal. As also there are not Three Uncreated nor Three Incomprehensibles, but One Uncreated and One Incomprehensible. So likewise the Father is Almighty, the Son Almighty, and the Holy Ghost Almighty. And yet they are not three Almighties, but One Almighty.

So the Father is God, and the Son is God, and the Holy Ghost is God. And yet there are not Three Gods, but One God. So likewise the Father is Lord, the Son is Lord, and the Holy Ghost is Lord. And yet not Three Lords but One Lord. For like as we are compelled by the Christian verity to acknowledge every Person by himself to be God and Lord, so are we forbidden by the Catholic religion to say, there be Three Gods or Three Lords. The Father is made of none, neither created, nor begotten. The Son is of the Father alone; not made nor created, but begotten. The Holy Ghost is

11

of the Father, and of the Son neither made, nor created nor begotten, but proceeding.

So there is One Father, not Three Fathers. One Son, not Three Sons. One Holy Ghost, not Three Holy Ghosts. And in this Trinity none is afore or after Another. None is greater or less than Another, but the whole Three Persons are Co-Eternal together and Co-Equal. So that in all things, as is aforesaid, the Unity in Trinity and the Trinity in Unity is to be worshipped. He therefore that will be saved, must thus think of the Trinity.

Furthermore, it is necessary to salvation that he also believe rightly the Incarnation of Our Lord Jesus Christ, The Son of God, is God and Man.

God, of the substance of the Father, begotten before the worlds, and made of the substance of His mother born in the world. Perfect God and Perfect Man, of a reasonable soul and human flesh subsisting. Equal to the Father as touching His God, and inferior to the Father as touching His manhood. Who although He be God and Man, yet He is not two, but One Christ. One, not by conversion of the Godhead into Flesh, but by taking of the manhood into God. One altogether, not by confusion of substance, but by Unity of Person. For as the reasonable soul and flesh is one man, so God and Man is One Christ. Who suffered for our salvation, descended into hell, arose again the third day from the dead. He ascended into Heaven, He sitteth on the right hand of the Father, God Almighty, from whence He shall judge the quick and the dead. At whose coming all men shall rise with their bodies and shall give account for their

12

own works. And they that have done good shall go into everlasting life, and they that have done evil into everlasting fire. This is the Catholic faith which except a man believe faithfully and firmly, he cannot be saved.

The Bute translation of this creed is that of a woman, whose translation has never been excelled. Many men have unsuccessfully attempted to surpass her. Her name was Lady Mary Mortley Montague, who married John Stuart, Marquis of Bute, and bore him fourteen children. Bute is a small island of Scotland, the seat of the Marquis being Mountstuart. John Stuart was a man of plain countenance, plain taste, and small ambition. George the Third through friendship, not merit, made him Prime Minister, in which place he found himself very much out-of-place. Totally unsuited to intrigue and artifice he became easy prey for his enemies, and retired from public life. Lady Mary was a witty and brilliant conversationalist, as well as a deep thinker and prolific authoress. History tells us that John Stuart loved his home. Too bad he did not care more for travel. His wife might have borne fewer children.

In my opinion, which is absolutely of no consequence, the Athanasian Creed should never have been excluded from our Prayer Book, because it depicts more clearly than any other document the mystery and relationship of the [three persons of the] Trinity.

In an old Prayer Book, brought from London to Jamestown in the late 1600's by my father's people,

I find some prayers which in nowise should have been omitted. I am positively chagrined at the loss of the following five, so sorely needed by every generation.

1. "A prayer for fools," reminding God that they don't know what they are doing.

2. "A prayer for the light-headed," asking God to impute not what he, or she, says, or does amiss.

3. "A prayer upon the necessity of sending for a physician," hoping to God that he, the physician, knows what he is doing.

4. "Ejaculations during childbirth," the equivalent of "Come down quick, Lord, and do something." I have often wondered just what women were supposed to do during childbirth, now I know. They should ejaculate.

5. And the last of the five is my pet one, "Prayer upon taking a physic," asking God "to act according to your strength and give you ease. Amen."

A fourth creed, rarely referred to, and of little historic church value, is the Henotican, published in 482. The mighty fall of the Roman Empire occurred in 476 and Constantinople outstripped Rome both in culture and in splendor. In 482 the churches of the East and the West again started a jealous free-for-all over the Trinity. The East said that "one of the Trinity died on the Cross." The West said that "one member of the Trinity suffered death upon the Cross." A man named Acacius, of Constantinople, decided like our Mr. Truman that he would just sit himself right down and write a letter saying what he thought. The Henotican was a

letter to the Pope. It was full of double talk. Acacius was a politician looking for a party. He was all things to all men. However, the majority of historians grant him the benefit of judgment as to why he was straddling the fence of the Trinity, saying that in this letter he was genuinely endeavoring to achieve a compromise between the Eastern and Western churches. Acacius was as generous as he was aggressive. He was the Bishop of Media and a very rich man in his own right of both maternal and paternal inheritance. He gave many possessions in order to feed and free seven thousand starving Persians.

Felix, who was then Pope, didn't like this letter. He sent an embassy to Acacius to bring him before him, to answer charges against himself. Acacius confiscated these papers of his summons, and had the embassy imprisoned. During their forced confinement he went every day to have a little talk with them. They signed the Hetrion which cost them their lives. Acacius says that they were converted to his way of thinking. There are many methods of persuasion when a man is behind bars.

When his embassy did not return, the Pope sent out his two-legged bloodhounds. They were the *akoimetoi* meaning "the sleepless." These boys were the ones to get the low-down on you. They were church detectives, or religious snoopers, an order of monks trained for investigation of secret motives, and they were allowed the employment of disguise, both male and female, to accomplish their purpose. "The sleepless" put the ecclesiastical bee on Acacius and buzzed him before the Pope.

The Emperor was a ruthless man, having come from a province of brigands and bandits. He was delighted to be of any service in persecuting one of higher birth and superior intellect. Acacius was condemned to death.

The last pretender to the throne of Creed Writers was John (Henley) born in Melton in 1692. He was the son of the rector of Melton and was himself the rector of Bloomsbury Chapel in London. He entered St. John's College at Cambridge when he was seventeen, and left it the same year. There was nothing there he did not know, and nothing they could ask him which he could not answer. So he told them all a "cheery-bye" and beat it. He attracted the largest crowds that ever gathered in an English-speaking church. He advertised his sermons, which was unheard of; he had his congregation remove their shoes to be comfortable and he preached without his pants to "wake them all up." For this he was arrested in 1746. At Communion he gave them three full cups of good stout wine. On Sunday he stuck to the Gospel but twice a week he lectured, and the sky was the limit. He let everything and everybody have it, in biting and riotous satire, and his buffoonery was accompanied by preposterous pantomime and mimicry. He edited a weekly journal of brilliant nonsense called the *HypDoctor* to which every sophisticate in England subscribed. He was riding so high that he thought he would write [for] himself, a creed, in prayer form, to do away with superfluous creeds and liven up a bit the good old one of the Apostles. If it was good enough for the men who had walked

18

with God, it was good enough for him. He founded a sect called the Henleyarians, but when he died, there was no one with the elasticity of mind and the religious clownery to succeed him. From his pen flowed the jest of much wisdom and satire of much worth. John Henley hated a hypocrite. You could take off your shoes, and take off your pants. Anything was alright, but being a hypocrite. When the Bishop chased him out of the church, he rented a place in Newport Market and kept on going strong.

The children of today are given, what seems to me, very little preparation for confirmation. Had you attended, fifty years ago, a school under the supervision of the church, you would have been brought into the church, before the altar and given a religious examination by a bevy of ministers, before you were considered ripe for confirmation. And unless you had studied, you could not pass it. Many failed and tried again. Candidates for confirmation were brought separately, one at a time, before these ministers and the Bishop, to be questioned. The clergymen sat at a table, but you stood, as you had been told to stand, with your heels touching, and your hands behind your back. The catechism was for babies, you thought. Those questions almost bored you. Then came the ones from both the Old and New Testaments. They were not easy ones, and they had better have been answered correctly, and I don't mean maybe. Some of these questions were worded, so as to require not only names and places, but to reveal an insight into your own reasoning. If you became pale or wobbled, you were allowed to seat yourself on a stool comprised of tin-can cylinders covered with carpet, with your pinafore pulled over your knees as far down as you could get it. No bare thighs and chapped hips in those days.

After the Bible questions came the big pay off. You were on your feet again to recite these three creeds word for word, and if you faltered, you just knew that your own minister, who was also your school principal, would want to boil you in oil. If you had done it in the classroom you could do it in the church, and if you expected some day to stand before Jesus, you could get some good practice right now by standing before the Bishop. When it was all over and you heard far-away, it seemed, voices saying "very good," you ran home as fast as you could to cry. At least I did.

Maybe it is just as well that this old-fashioned rigid training of children has been abolished. It often turned the tender years into very harsh ones. But this hardness of requirement encrusted them with religious armor invulnerable to any later attack of indecision or unbelief, to which the associations and circumstances of life are obliged to subject us all.

All of us are much concerned over our children becoming a worldly success, in the eyes of men, during a life service which we know will end. For this purpose we are willing to exhaust our energy and our means. Wouldn't it be a wonderful world to live in, if parents had exercised the same concern for their children becoming a success, in the eyes of God, during a life service that will not end? We know that training is the main preparation for achievement. Yet we sit here, while in the public schools, which we accept as standards of citizenship, there is, for the acknowledgment of God, not even a prayer. And still we sit.

To hold the security of our nation fast, we need an army. To make a soldier of a man we give him equipment—the best. We drill him over and over in what he must know to save his life. We see to it that he is afforded, by intelligent experts, the opportunity to know and to demonstrate this knowledge, before he reaches the firing line. In an army a man moves shoulder to shoulder with others of equal interest, and when he is wounded every known aid is rushed to him. In regard to him we remember everything but the sixth commandment. So much for the material which is all temporal. But what about the spiritual, which is eternal?

To hold fast the security of the Church, we need Christians. But when a man would become a Christian he is surely on his own. The equipment we donate is the discard of our secondary thinking. After everything else has been thought of and attended to, our drilling of him, if there is any, is done sitting down. The few experts who could help him are behind seminary doors where he has no contact with them, unless he be enrolled to be counted among the ordained. He moves shoulder to shoulder in his daily maneuvers with others of lax, or no, interest in religion. When he is wounded by vicissitude, and the blood of cold and hunger and disease flows from his vitals and drains his spirit, the majority of us give him no aid, saying

21

that after all we have charitable agencies, let them worry. The agencies do finally do something, maybe, after the red tape of investigation is unrolled and they are sure, first, that there are sufficient funds to pay the salaries of their own staff. The firing line of life begins with the cradle and extends to the grave. The victory of Christianity is the saving of a soul, but the Christian call to arms, in comparison to what it should be, is such a low whisper that God must have to lean very far out of heaven even to hear it, here on earth.

The Christians who are making a verbal flourish of concern about religion but never leaving their four walls to do anything about it remind me of something I witnessed one morning at 2:30 A.M. Next door to me, there was a so-called nursing home, operated by a thin-lipped and bedraggled sadist who flapped a filthy feather duster around in shabby rooms papered with bold and fierce designs. This place was a haven for drunks, and a refuge for unwanted relatives, suffering from the pathetic lapse of mental vitality which often accompanies advanced age. Directly across from my own bedroom, was a room in which was confined one of Louisville's most notorious, rather than famous, criminal lawyers. When you engaged him, the public knew both that you were guilty and were sure of acquittal. His light came on at 2:30 in the morning and shone through his window, across to mine, and in my face. I raised up, and this is what I saw. Arising from off his bed, he removed his pajamas. Then he yawned and stretched, scratching himself a bit here and there,

22

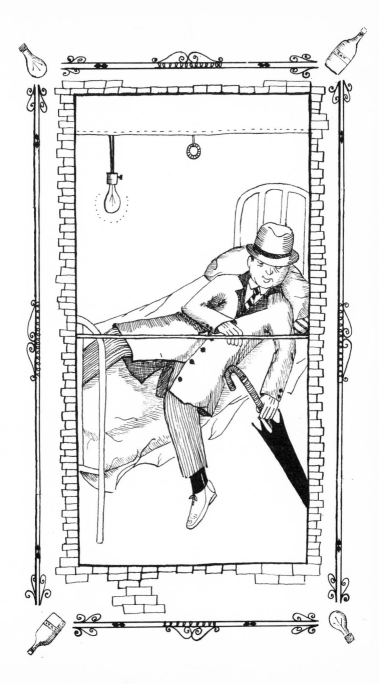

and striding about his room he made me think of Adam in his garden. Always eager for adventure, even at 2:30 A.M., I did not lower my shade. This manipulator of juries put on his underwear, his socks, his pants, his shoes, his tie, his coat, his overcoat, his hat, his gloves; then taking up his umbrella he fell back into bed, pulled up the covers, and turned out his light.

God forbid that we Christians fall back on our beds of inactivity and pulling up our covers of indifference, turn out our light of endeavor.

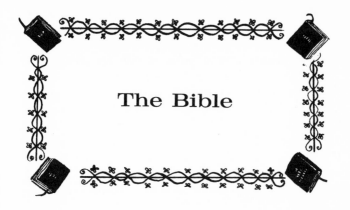

The Bible

Jesus tells us to "search the Scriptures." Those of you who merely read the Bible and find it dull or mystifying have yet to study it. Many people say that they do not understand it. Men do not at first understand the written pages of a language unknown to them, without a single word giving them any clue as to its meaning. Yet if any man is sufficiently interested to want to know what those pages say and mean, he diligently goes about the systematic and serious study of it. No subject can be comprehended in any other manner, and man's individual intelligence suffices as a scale whereby that comprehension is measured.

The Bible is a storehouse of individual spiritual revelation and release. It appeals to every class, taste, and mood. It depicts king and pauper; saint and sinner. It is tragic, and humorous. It is violent, and gentle. It is proud, and meek. It is beseeching, and triumphant. It contains every emotion, every temptation, every ambition, every aspiration; all of the wisdom and all of the foolishness of every type of man. If you are grieved, or ill, or confused, or troubled, or even bored, go to your Bible and study it. Take Jesus' advice and "search it." If it means nothing to you at first, keep at it, and if you do, almost suddenly you will come to see and understand many things which in the duration of a lifetime could never have been satisfactorily explained to you by someone else. Through this searching, you will come as near as it is possible, here in this life, to becoming of one mind with God.

The preservation, as well as the recording, of the Scriptures belongs to the Jews. There was born, in Rome, a man named Jerome, who became the ardent student of all Holy Writ. Later this man became a monk, heading four large monasteries built by him with the fabulous wealth given him by a woman named Paula, who was in love with him, and whom he refused to marry. The largest of these retreats was at Bethlehem where he died. Jerome spent his life translating, from Hebrew and Greek, the ordained Scriptures that Jesus told men to "search," and when he had finished them, he was buffeted by seeing the Christians meet in the Council at Carthage, and in their smug bigotry, discard and throw on the ash heap of history the books of Esdras one and two, Tobias, Judith, additions to Esther, Prayer of Manasses, Maccabees one and two, Acts of St. Paul, "the Shepherd" of Hermas, and mind you now, even the Apocalypse of

Peter, the one selected, and designated, by Christ to found the Church. These books, thrown by the Christians into intended oblivion, are known as the Apocrypha, meaning "hidden." Between Greece and Rome there had already started in the Church the creeping paralysis of disgusting difference and dispute. The Roman Church had the religious appreciation to retain some of these discarded works in their Bible. They are included in the Vulgate, and are found in the Old Testament.

There was also born at Rome a man named Polycarp, who witnessed the Crucifixion, and became the disciple and companion of John. This man's literary works comprise a crescending triumph ending in an almost unparalleled spiritual finale. The works of Polycarp give to some people an even truer picture of Christ than do the four Gospels.

The Church having severed the inspired word of God, the English Reformers maimed it further. They retranslated it and threw out the Vulgate.

It is a tragic pity that the Reformation could not have been the Conformation, or even the Confirmation. The revolt of a priest named Martin Luther against indulgences sold in the Church was a righteous movement, but it became infiltrated with the foul and murderous purposes of vicious people to attain their own gain. Henry the Eighth dragged an empire into bloody .rebellion because of his lustful appetite for a woman. Married to Catherine of Aragon, the daughter of Ferdinand and Isabella, he desired to be rid of her. Her barrenness was his alibi. The Reformation was his loophole. As Thomas Wolsey, his chancellor, had been unsuccessful in obtaining papal sanction for the King's divorce, Henry denounced the Pope and proclaimed himself the head of the English Church. With his excommunication papers nailed to the Cathedral doors, he married the luscious and shamelessly ambitious Anne Boleyn. This beauteous babe's backside reposed on her throne chair a short three years, then, off came her head. Lover Boy Henry was sniffing the scented tresses of his next victim.

Don't think for a minute that the Protestants were not as egotistically bigoted as the Mother Church. To cement English regard and elevation, a corps of translators under King James I retranslated the Bible and threw out the Vulgate. How many of you have wondered, or taken the few minutes to find out what type of man this James was? It would be both apropos and rather soothing for me to tell you that James was a devout man, and a worthy King. He was neither. He was a degenerate.

Sired by the very good looking, but equally good-for-nothing Lord Darnley, James was born of Mary, Queen of Scots. He joined the ranks of his mother's assassins and saw his daughter beggared and exiled, and gave her no aid. James' learning became a mockery to his tutor, the able and brilliant George Buchanan, who hoped to make an author of James, and cultivated in him the flare he showed for writing. But this flare backfired in Buchanan's face. James' talent for writing became grossly deformed by offensive and exag-

gerated superstition, witches and demons being the chief topics on which he dwelled. This man's clumsy person and his gross manners, made him the unfavorable object of his subject, whose disrespect for him was further augmented by his, shall we say, repulsive fondness for masculine favorites of distinguished personal beauty. This alone is enough to cloud his name. Women who stamp themselves as respectable have learned to tolerate, and even accept, the immorality of men, but not even a man will stand for another man's unsavory practice which is so unmoral, as not even fit to be called immoral. If some of you do not know what I have told you, you may think why in heavens name doesn't she keep her big mouth shut. Why tell us this, and introduce a decaying element of spoil? Precisely the opposite is my intention. I am trying to make you see that God's word is His Own, and not men's. Though it be mauled about, by hand and mouth, by liars, thieves, murderers, adulterers or hypocrites, it is still the imperishable and non-contaminable word of the Creator. It will survive all time, all races, all creeds, as well as all filth, and all religious erosion.

The Bible is almost a primer in comparison to the vast store and wealth of recorded religious thinking. The more you study, naturally the more you learn. But strangely enough, the more you learn, the less you know. If you suspect yourself of becoming unstable, or dubious, it is just as well, in your case, to let it all go, and stick to the bedrock certainty that God loves you and will always be with you, unless you, by wilful and defiant rebel-

lion, separate yourself from Him. But your voluntary separation of yourself from God can only be
conduct-deep. Regardless of what you are, or what
you do, the very fact that you can draw your breath
proves God's cooperative assertion of your existence. No mode of thought, or condition of living,
can dissolve parenthood. God is your Father. You
are His Child, and whether you will it or not, He
still loves you. The benefits and grace of God are
obtained by your love of Him, but His love for
you is unchanging and everlasting.

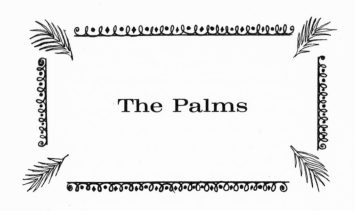

The Palms

Ash Wednesday is the first day of Lent, whose beginning was purposely placed on the center day of the week; indicative of looking both at the days that are past and the days that are to come; [of] seeking God's forgiveness for that which is behind us, and asking His guidance in that which is before us.

The word Lent comes from the word "lencten" meaning "a new beginning." The prefix "Ash" originated from the practice of sprinkling ashes on the heads of the penitent. After the first Palm Sunday the refuse collectors of the Jerusalem streets piled the withered and trampled palm branches outside the city's walls, and set fire to them. After the Crucifixion, the believers in the Galilean who had died went to the ash heap and, kneeling, made with the ashes, the sign of the cross on their foreheads. Jerome, Leo, and Augustine all affirm, and assure us, that the office of Lent was instituted by the Apostles themselves, and was made obligatory in the Church in the year 250 A.D.

On Ash Wednesday bread was baked and kept until the following year, at which time it was doled out, in morsels, as medicine. After two thousand years we think that we have discovered something new. Our own penicillin is nothing more than mold from bread, made sterile in liquid and in tablet form.

The symbolical usage of Holy Water can also be traced to the Apostles, who carried it on their persons in small vials and, when visiting in homes, used it as a means of healing and benediction, by the method of sprinkling it about. With the ad-mixture of salt, which represented life-giving and preserving qualities, this water was blessed yearly on the day before the Resurrection, then sealed for opportune administration. Holy Water was, and still is, drunk twice yearly in the Greek Church: at midnight Christmas Mass, and at Epiphany.

During the services held by the Apostles, a candlestick supporting 15 candles was lit. Fourteen for the 14 Prophets who predicted the coming of the Messiah, and the fifteenth for Christ Himself. These services were held always in the evening. On the last Friday in Lent, or Crucifixion Day, the service was silent. The prayers were silent. No bells were rung, and no musical instrument sounded. This service was called "creeping to the cross." Gathering in single file outside the church the people, on entering, went forward on their knees to kiss the altar cross, placed within reach of their lips.

Creeping is still practiced in the Latin Church. On attending Christmas Mass in Mexico City in the largest Cathedral in the Western Hemisphere, which took ninety-six years to build, I found all benches removed from the church, and everyone on their knees. My dwindling knowledge of Latin conveyed to me very little of what was being chanted, and being a "pagan Protestant" I was sufficiently spiritually weak to be obliged to brace myself against a pillar. As my shoulders grew heavier and heavier against the pillars of support, I thought of poor old Samson. After one hour of this I made my Protestant exit practically on all fours.

Henry VIII issued a proclamation forcing the English Church to keep this custom of creeping to the cross; saying, "creeping to the crosse signifyeth an humblynge of ourselfe to Christe before the crosse, and the kyssnge of it a memorie of our redemption made upon the crosse."

If this Old Brother had confined his creeping and his kissing within the church, with only spiritual intent, the guillotine would have severed fewer heads from off their fair necks. Henry was not only an exponent of the literal kiss, but was an advocate of the figurative one also, in that he let the Pope know that as far as he was concerned he, the Pope, could kiss his, Henry's, foot.

The duration of Lent is forty days, and contrary to what is commonly believed was not intended solely in commemoration of the forty days fast of

Jesus in the wilderness. This number of days set apart by the Apostles included also the forty days of the deluge, the forty years of wandering of the Jews, the forty days repentance granted the Ninevites, and the forty days fast of both Moses and Elias.

Mid-Lent, or Passion Sunday, was originally called "Carl Sunday." A carling was a dried vegetable resembling both a pea and a bean. This food was passed and eaten in the church on this mid-Lenten Sunday. The beans were symbolic of confession, and the soaking process, before cooking, represented the necessary softening of the heart. A manuscript in the Ashmolean Museum refers to this custom, and to this dish as "Lenten stuff." From the *Quadragesimale Spirituale,* written in Paris in 1565, is this quotation: After the sallad eaten in Lent, we eat fried beans, by which we understand confession. When we would have beans well sodden, we lay them in steepe (to soften their hearts) otherwise they would never seeth kindly. Therefore if we purpose to mend our faults, it is not sufficient barely to confess them at all adventure, but we must let our confession lie in steepe in the water of meditation. In the light verse of the ancient Colin Clout we find some lines on how "the penitent, in his fast of Lenten carlings, looks to when he may be loosed upon a pigge."

In reference to Lent, the Greek Church has always been more strict than the Latin, and has enforced this office with each season, or four times a year. The Protestant churches which recognize Lent have left its manner and degree of observance entirely to individual conscience and judgment. This, to me, seems a pity, because this attitude is obliged to generate indifference. Twenty-five or thirty years seems a very short time to us who are adult, yet in that length of time or little more, every one of us will be gone, and those who will take our places are now the children. In one generation the world could become almost any-thing we choose to make it, by planting in the childhood of the world the seed we would have grow. The child who is denied the privilege of ob-serving Lent has been deprived of lasting self-im-provement through voluntary self-sacrifice. He has had removed from him a yearly opportunity, in spiritual growth, to understand, the only phase of Jesus' life which we are entitled to share with Him. We are not born of virgins. No dove descends upon our heads when we are baptized. We cannot raise the dead, and the earth will not quake when we draw our last breath. Meditation and self-sacrifice are the only things in life we can share with Jesus, and it is not blasphemy when we claim equality with Him in the privilege of approach to God through prayer. Lent is the season of prayer, and prayer is the lifeline between God and man, an unbreakable cable of saving Grace.

Lent to us may have an uninteresting and in-glorious beginning, but it has a comforting and majestic ending. In the Resurrection is the asser-tion of visible and undisputed truth and proof that life does not end with the grave, but rather begins with a rebirth of lasting spiritual splendor.

We enter the world through the miracle of birth.

Everything in life has on it God's price tag and must be paid for either by ourselves, or someone else. Even Jesus was not exempt. For the redemption of the world He was required by God, to pay with His life. The price of birth is the suffering of our mother and her blood, in which we were bathed, was a necessary contribution that we might have life.

We enter the Kingdom of Heaven by the miracle of death. Emerging from the womb of the grave we are reborn. The price of this rebirth is the suffering of Jesus, the Christ, and His blood which flowed from the cross was a necessary contribution that we might, through salvation, have life everlasting. Blood is the symbol of life, both temporal and eternal. It is also a symbol of sacrifice, without which, there can be nothing of any worth.

The emblem of Lent is the palm branch, and it would be unfitting, and unworthy of it, for me not to call to your attention the importance of the palm tree to the people of Our Lord's generation. Because of its majesty and its many uses, it became emblematic of Judea, and its branch appeared on their coins. The different species of palm ranged from humble proportion to a height of over 100 feet. There was the date palm, furnishing fruit. There was the coconut palm, supplying both milk and food. There was the wine palm, from which flowed a vinous sap of spirituous liquor. There was the sugar palm, which was beaten and ground into very, very sweet sugar. The tender leaves of the palm were boiled as cabbage, affording a vegetable. The roots contained tannin and when brewed made a fragrant and refreshing drink. The sago palm supplied a strong starch. The pith of the palm was ground into flour from which was made the holy, or unleavened bread. The branches of the palm served as thatch for habitation.

The coarse fiber of the bark was used to make brooms and baskets, and mats. From the wood was carved utensils, bowls, spoons, and ladles. From the fine fiber of the leaves was made thread, used to stitch and sew. From the fiber of the giant palms were made ropes to anchor ships. The finest resin in the world, used by trapeze artists and acrobats, comes from the waxy, gluey issue of the palm. This substance is dark red, and is known as "dragon's blood," and called by this name among circus people. Palm oil, sweet in taste and yellow in color, was eaten as butter, and made into soap and candles. The timber of the palm tree is especially adaptable to massive building, being durable and free from rot. It is resistant to salt water which made it especially desirable for the construction of sea-going craft.

The seed of the Palm was eaten as a nut, and its tender kernels, when soaked in water, rendered a potent liniment for the aching muscles of both men and beasts. When these seeds are dried, they become transparent and as hard as ivory. They were carved into beads, and trinkets and heads for canes and staffs. The flower of the palm tree is yellowish-white, a very large cone-shaped blossom composed of many single flowers. The odor of the palm flower is much like our sweet violet, and its intense fra-.

grance can be detected at a great distance. From this blossom was distilled exotic perfume.

At the season of Jesus' entry into Jerusalem the palm trees were in full flower, and when the people strewed before Him their palm branches, it was a tribute of their most treasured possession, representing both their need and their luxury. When the savage tribes of these far-away tropic countries would destroy the subsistence of their enemies, and leave them desolate, they cut away their palm trees.

To the Jews the palm tree represented a blessing from Heaven, and was associated with the Chosen Ones of God. Any rabbi will, or should, tell you that the oil of anointment was the oil of the palm.

On the next Palm Sunday when a bit of palm branch is given you, do not regard it as a reminder of triumphant waving. If you remember the material uses it represented to those who first offered it, it should present to you the burning question of what have you offered the Galilean. Many of us calling ourselves His followers, are willing to give little of our luxury, and none of our need.

The people in that first Palm Sunday procession, who brought no palms themselves, yet joined in the marching and singing, remind me of the people who are basking in the benefits of the Church, but who have no idea of suffering any inconvenience to themselves in regard to its cause or purpose. The Church has baptized them. She has married them, and will bury them when they are dead. For them, the Church is a most urgently dependable and conveniently accommodating institution to

supply their own respectable necessity. As far as the real goal of the Church, well, that's too much for them, and while they are busy with their own affairs poor old God will have to get along as best He can. Of course the Church is an object of their revered affection. Surely no one doubts their loving regard for it. The ladies are so sweet, so polite; some of them so pretty, and so witty, and so clever. And the preacher is so cute. They just love him. But let the sweet ladies, or the cute minister ask them to do something, and as of that split second, they become so busy that they really haven't time to voice the refusal, that they just know is sure to be understood.

God grant that we may be moved to bring into His Church, and for its cause, some form of our own palm branch.

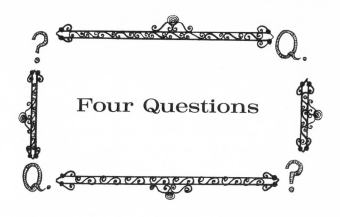

Four Questions

Almighty Lord, and everlasting God, vouchsafe we beseech Thee to direct, sanctify and govern, both our hearts and bodies, in the ways of Thy laws, and in the works of Thy commandments; that, through Thy most mighty protection, both here and ever, we may be preserved in body and soul, through our Lord and Saviour, Jesus Christ.

We are gathered here today in commemoration of the saddest day in the history of the entire world. The physical death of the Son of God. This is the man who, for three years, went about doing good. Three years of telling men who He was, and why He was here, and these same men repaid miracle and blessing with insult and murder, because they did not understand.

All of us, both rich and poor, both prince and pauper, are daily approaching one common, inescapable goal—the grave. When we are young life

43

seems so long, and death so far away. As we grow older, the certainty of dying becomes more real to us. When we are old, life seems so short, and we begin to wonder what will happen when we stand face to face with God. It is then that our parentage, however favored we may have been, our education, our privileges, our advantages, our possessions and our success, will become as much nothing as if they had never existed. The Bible tells us exactly what will happen. All of us will be resurrected, and separated as we are judged. The righteous will be gathered into the arms of God, and the wicked will be cast into Hell fire.

This place of everlasting damnation is becoming more and more unpopular with some people, and they resent being reminded of it. Such people like to go through their Bible, and pick out what they want to believe, what it suits them to believe. They just love to hear about Heaven, but when you talk about Hell, they want you to hurry up, and shut up.

Concerning the Judgment, we wonder just what will constitute the separation of the righteous from the wicked. Will we be obliged to stand there before the bar of God, and hear bared everything we ever said, thought, felt, or did? Not at all. Jesus tells us that we will be judged according to the works done in the flesh. In the flesh means while we lived upon the earth, and works means deeds, not, what was our faith or creed. Not, if and where we went to church, or what we believed or thought, or what we intended to do, or what we would like to have done, but what we actually did do. Then we ask ourselves just what do men do that makes them wicked, or righteous? This also Jesus answers for us, and prepares us for, ahead of time. Only four questions will be asked us. Jesus Himself will do the asking and it will be He who will pronounce the verdict of whether we will hear, "Come unto me," or "Depart from me." Jesus was once flesh and blood Himself. He lived here on the earth, as both child and man. He knows all of our weaknesses and temptations, because He has experienced them. And God, in His mercy and complete fairness, is going to let Jesus be our judge.

The first question our Lord will ask us will be "Whom have you seen hungry and thirsty and given food and drink?" Did you ever hear a knock on your door and find there a man who told you that he was hungry? And if so what did you do about it? You might want to ask me, if I am talking about bums and tramps. If that is what you want to call them, they are exactly those I am talking about. The unfortunates, the victims of circumstances, who are just as much children of God, as we. If we turn away any hungry man, we have turned away the Christ. Jesus tells us positively that "Inasmuch as ye have done it unto the least of these my brethren, ye have done it unto Me."

Now there are many kinds of hunger and thirst in the world, besides physical hunger and thirst which can be satisfied with material food and drink. There is loneliness that hungers for just a little of someone's time. The hunger of wondering if anyone cares can be fed with a little kindness.

Many men and women are not only hungry but actually starved for some affection from a nagging wife, or just one word of praise from a grouchy and fault-finding husband. Then there is the gnawing hunger of remorse, the realization, too late, of what we have left undone, one example being to look in the face of a dead mother, and suddenly to be reminded that we let her live out all of her days, without letting her know how much we loved her. Many people hunger and thirst for appreciation, and upon the tables of many lives we can place the food of gratitude. Jesus has told us that He is the Bread of Life and that His is the Water of Life, of which if we drink we never thirst again.

The second question will be "Whom have ye seen naked and clothed?" There hangs on our rear clothes closet poles enough discarded and seldom used clothing to cover every ragged and shabby person who needs them. But there is another form of nakedness which has no relation to the garments which cover our bodies. There is the nakedness of seeming failure which exposes our woe, when we have tried so hard and seem to be getting nowhere. It is then that we need someone to wrap about us the security of hope, and the incentive to try again. The nakedness of drunkenness and crime needs to be clothed with constructive help, to promote decency and self-respect. The nakedness of frustration and maladjustment needs the covering and protection of clear thinking and calm meditation. If we can help these people to but touch the hem of the robe of Christ,

46

they may be imbued with His virtue and transformed in life and purpose.

The third question will be "Whom have you as a stranger taken in?" There are many other ways of administering to a stranger than asking him inside your door to rest himself. A much grander way is to extend to all men who are strangers, the key to your heart and mind. There are strangers to your own opinion. Grant them the privilege of their own thinking, without argument. There are strangers to faith, and to belief. Do not belittle theirs, nor set your own above it. All faith is worthy in the eyes of God. There are strangers to modes of baptism, and customs of worship. Allow without criticism and bickering to every man his own. There are strangers to education and culture. Remember that learning comes from books, but that wisdom comes from God. Often the humble and uneducated man has more innate understanding than his brother with many degrees. No fool, is as big a fool, as the overly educated one, who thinks that he knows it all.

There are juvenile strangers in our courts, victims of neglect and broken homes, the hostages of selfishness. There are throngs of still smaller children in orphanages. Many of them will really never know just who they are, but will be lifelong strangers to themselves. There are strangers of race, men of different color of skin, whose flesh, and bone, and blood and feelings are identical with our own. There are strangers and misplaced persons among us today, exiles, driven from home, trying to make a new life. You may have a stranger of opinion, and motive, in your own household. If you have, consider his or her point of view. Don't tell your husband that he is working in the wrong place, and should change his job. Leave that to him. It is his job. Don't insist that your son be a lawyer, or a doctor, where he has no natural bent to be either. One may long to plow a field, or navigate a ship. It is his life that he must live. Don't try to select a husband for your daughter. It is she who is going to live with him, not you. And if our children make a mistake and make the wrong choice, don't reproach them. It is our duty to stand by them and to help them. They are no less our children when they are forty, than they were when they were four. Sometime by our words and actions we estrange from ourselves those whom we love the very most.

God help us to take in every stranger, under the shelter of our sympathy, our confidence, our understanding, and our help, each one according to his own individual need.

The fourth question will be "Whom have you seen sick and visited in prison?" How many of us have ever visited a prison, or cared what goes on inside, or what happens to those who are confined there? How many of us are willing or have tried to do anything about making things better for prisoners? One of the major poets has truthfully said "Stone walls do not a prison make, nor iron bars, a cage." There is the sickness of mind, and of soul, as well as of body [that imprisons individuals]. And there is the prison of a broken spirit, surrounded by walls of poverty, disease, slander, abuse, and injustice. The ladder of God needs to be let down along these walls, a ladder upon which these inmates may climb, rung by rung, with our help until they are free to behold a new horizon of spiritual escape. Church-going is good and right and deserves to be highly commended, but after we leave our Sabbath pews there are six other days to be lived before we return. Will we leave the faith we profess there on the church bench, or will we take it with us, those other six days, into our home, our office, our shop, and factory, to be used for the Glory of God, and for the extension of His Kingdom?

Everything that we do and say registers some sort of impression upon those with whom we come in contact. Are we going about spreading a doctrine of resentment, bitterness, reproach, complaint, and self-interest; or, are we, by our own lives, expounding a gospel of tolerance, patience, and understanding? Even common politeness has an engulfing force of comfort in the world.

Once, a long time ago, I was sent away to a very expensive school. I expected something exciting and very fancy. I thought that I was going to have myself one big time, but I found things very different from what I had expected. I found in that school things of lasting worth; the combination of simple truth and unbiased thinking. Above the classroom door was a motto in large gold letters. After all of these years, I can still see it. It read, "Politeness is to do and say the kindest thing in the kindest way."

Let us again pray: Lord of all power and might,

Who art the author and giver of all good things, graft in our hearts the love of Thy name. Increase in us true religion and in Thy great mercy keep us in the same. Stir up in us the will to bring forth the fruits of good works. This we ask in the name of Jesus Christ, Our Lord. Amen.

The following is the daily prayer of St. Francis of Assisi: Lord make me an instrument of thy peace; where there is hatred, let me sow love; where there is injury, pardon; where there is doubt, faith; where there is despair, hope; where there is darkness, light; and where there is sadness, joy. O Divine Master, grant that I may not so much seek to be consoled as to console; to be understood, as to understand; to be loved, as to love; for it is in giving that we receive, it is in pardoning that we are pardoned, and it is in dying that we are born to eternal life. Amen.

The following is the Inaugural prayer of George Washington: Almighty God, we make our earnest prayer that Thou wilt keep the United States in Thy Holy protection. That Thou wilt incline the hearts of the citizens to cultivate a spirit of obedience, and to entertain a brotherly affection and love for one another, as fellow citizens. May we be pleased to do justice, to love mercy, and to conduct ourselves in charity, humility, and gentle temper of mind, which were the characteristics of the Divine Author of our blessed religion, and without whose humble example we can never hope to be a happy nation. Grant us our supplication through Jesus Christ our Lord. Amen.

And here is the death cell prayer of Mary, Queen

of Scots before she walked to place her head on the executioner's block at the decree of her own cousin, who was also a woman:

Keep us, oh God, from all smallness. Let us be large in thought, in word, and in deed. Let us have done with complaint, and leave off all self-seeking. May we put away all pretense, and meet each other with pity and without prejudice. May we never be hasty in Judgment of others. Make us always generous. Let us take time to be calm and gentle. Teach us to put into action our better impulses, and to walk unafraid. Grant that we may realize that the little things of life are those which create our differences, and that in the big things of life, we are as one under God. And, O Lord, let us never forget to be kind. Amen.

The preceding prayers of these so different people of varied race, creed and generation prayed hundreds of years apart, prove our "oneness" under God.

For some of us life seems to be an uphill drag, as we bear our own cross. Everyone, if he or she, reaches maturity has a cross. Some crosses can be seen, but often invisible ones are the heaviest, and most heart-breaking ones of all. And it is not until we surmount our own problems, under God, and reach the top of our hill, that we can look about us, and clearly see our God-willed purpose. The hills of the earth seem to have been purposely chosen, by God, as markers of faith. The commandments were given to men atop one mountain, and the Ark rested on another. Jesus was transfigured on a Mount and there the curtains of

Heaven were drawn back. Both the Crucifixion, and the Ascension took place upon a hilltop and the most soul-stirring message ever delivered, has been called the Sermon on the Mount. It is only after we have borne our cross all of the way up the steep sides of life that we find the glory of God.

The hours of the day in which we are gathered together here, represent the last of the three hours on the cross. All of you are familiar with the hatred of Herod, and the treachery and double-talk of Pilate. The Son of God died for every man that ever was, or will be, born. The Redemption of the world was His only purpose. For this cause He was born, and for this cause He died. He died for you. Some of you may wonder just how you know when, or if, you are saved. You need not wonder any more, because you are already saved, if you, through repentance, will accept your salvation. Your salvation awaits you right there where it was purchased for you, at the Cross. No one else can go after it, or bring it to you, regardless of how much they may love you. You must go to the Cross for it yourself.

This gift of God required too big a price to be laid about carelessly. To obtain this priceless treasure there must be two keys. God has one, and you have the other, [operating] on the same principle as a lock box at the bank. One key is yours and one is the bank's. Yours is always available to you, but it takes the two, working together, to get at your treasure. Your key to salvation is the key to repentance, and if it is real and true your key will fit. It is then that God matches your key with His own which is the key of forgiveness. God waits at the Cross for your repentance. He wants to forgive you, and He promises that He will cast your sins as far away as the heavens are from the earth, and that He will remember them no more. It is your repentance, and God's merciful and ready forgiveness, that grants and establishes your Salvation. No man need ever feel that he is too steeped in sin for the benediction of God's grace and forgiveness.

Some of the greatest saints were once the blackest sinners. Moses was once a murderer. He slew an Egyptian, and hid him in the sand. David was once an adulterer. To satisfy his lust he took away the wives of three men. Jacob was once both liar and thief. At the instigation of an unprincipled mother, he deceived his blind and aged father in order to wrest from him the birthright belonging to his brother, Esau.

No seemingly minor offense can become so major as the jealousy of children, fed by the favoritism of a parent. Because our children are different, it is natural that we should observe them differently, because each of them represents to us something apart from the others. One is more talented, another is more generous, while yet another may be more dependable, or more trustworthy. One may swell our pride, while another stirs our pity. But to love one more than another is both wicked and cruel. Peter after denying His Lord three times became the bedrock of the Church. Mary of Magdala was once a harlot; not a foolish and overly romantic woman, who had loved a man unwisely, and been betrayed by him; but a public prostitute, as filthy in mind as in body. Yet the forgiveness and saving grace of God rendered her fit to stand at her dying Saviour's feet, along with His Mother and St. John. It was to this forgiven woman-of-sin that Our Lord made His first appearance after He was resurrected. No man, or woman, has ever been, or ever will be, too evil for God to behold with mercy and certain forgiveness. And it is never too late to ask for this forgiveness. The crucified thief, named Dismas, turned to Jesus when he was dying, and was promised the paradise of God. What a tragic pity that men like Dismas are ready to die before they learn and live, and are ready to do what is right, and could not enjoy, while they yet lived, the blessings of God. Life is like a storehouse filled with all manner of things and we may have anything there that is within our reach. The things of the greatest value are not found on the highest shelves.

We extend our arms to give our blood to the wounded, the ill, and the dying. In our blood are the saving elements of transfusing temporal life. The Son of God extended his arms, on the beams of a dogwood cross, to give to us, His blood, which serves as an everflowing stream of saving grace. Blood containing the divine elements of transfusion to insure everlasting life in His—God's Kingdom— prepared by Him, for us, before the beginning of the world. As long as you live, every time you see a cross against the sky, remember that Jesus died for you. You hear a great deal today about preparedness, and the importance of training, in this, that, and the other. After a man studies that which he selects, and finishes his training in various trades, or vocations, he is given a certificate, or diploma, or degree. This, he tells himself is all that he needs to see him through. The things of the world are important to us here, and they have their rightful places. But the things of the world will all pass away. Often we neglect the most important thing that will not pass away—our soul.

In this life, which precedes the life to come, God has not neglected to endow us with something that we cannot learn from any book, or be given by any instructor. It serves as the diploma or degree of God, rendering us prepared to live [His life]. We do not have to labor, nor study to acquire it. It is His gift to us. We are born with it. It is holy, indisputable, and unfailing. It is all any man needs. It is our conscience. It is God's direction of us. It is always with us, and if we obey its voice, we can never be wrong. It is the chart and the compass of life, whose needle points to the Glory of God. Our conscience can be the gentle whisper of a guardian angel, or it can become the thunder and lightning warning of that indescribable something of kinship with God which men call their soul. All of the knowledge that is contained in the libraries of the world is as nothing in comparison to this, God's direction of us. He has promised us that He will never leave or forsake us, and in this, His gift of our conscience, He makes this promise true.

If any one of you believed that there was no life after death, and that Salvation was a lot of bunk, you wouldn't be seated here today. If any of you are doubtful concerning your own salvation, you can leave this chapel today, knowing that you are saved. All that you have to do is, later as we pray, to bow your heart and your head, and ask God to forgive you for any wrong you may have done, and to help you to do better. He does not care who you are, what you may be now, nor what you might ever have done.

When you go home, get your Bible and place it beside your bed. Every morning, before you put on your clothes, get into the habit of opening it, and reading it even if it is just one verse. It will only take a few seconds. Open it at random, any place the pages fall apart, then read and it will amaze you how often the words before you will apply to you on that very day. Don't be fearful of what, of how much, God expects of you. All that He asks of any of us is to do each day, the very best we can. When the whole thing is boiled down, that is all that there is to it. The good Samaritan was not a man who sat and wondered what he could do to please God, neither did he go from place to place hunting something to do. He was a simple man of kindly mercy, who did what he saw needed to be done in connection with those he came upon, on his own way through life. Yet Jesus paid him the highest tribute of worthy living.

God has mercifully and wisely spaced the span of our lives at just one day at a time. Yesterday is past and gone. There is nothing that we can do about it. It can never be recalled. Tomorrow we may never see, and if and when we do, it, too, will then be just today. Surely we can live with decency and honor and truth for just one day at a time, taking just one step at a time, until we reach the Kingdom of Heaven.

Religion was not intended as a long-faced conclusion to curb your pleasures, and to make you, and all about you, miserable. True religion is a happy and contagious trend of thinking that betters every phase of your daily life and helps you to enjoy it to the fullest.

Let us pray: "Almighty and everlasting God, Who of Thy tender love for mankind, has sent Thy Son, Our Saviour Jesus Christ, to take upon Himself one flesh, and to suffer death upon the cross, help us to follow the example of His patience, that we may be partakers of His Resurrection. Thou who hast promised forgiveness of sins, to all who with true repentance and steadfast faith turn unto Thee, have mercy upon us. Pardon and deliver us from all of our sins. Confirm and strengthen us in all goodness, and bring us to everlasting life, through Jesus Christ, Our Lord. Amen." And now "may the peace of God which passeth all understanding, keep our hearts and minds in the knowledge and love of God, and of His Son, Jesus Christ Our Lord. Forgive us, and bless us, and help us this day and forever more. Amen."

"Almighty God, look with Divine pity upon all people, everywhere. Defend us with Thy truth. Protect us with Thy love. Deliver us from violence. Help us to find Thy way. Strengthen us to fulfill Thy purpose. This we ask in the name of Jesus, Thy Only Son, Our Lord. Amen."

Among the Psalms are found these words: Wilt not Thou, O God, give us help from trouble, for vain is the help of man. Then they cried unto the Lord in their troubles and he brought them out of their distresses. Bow down Thy ear, O Lord, and hear us, for I am needy. In the day of my trouble I will call upon Thee, and Thou wilt answer. I have eaten my bread as ashes, and mingled my drink with weeping. Thou wilt show me the path of life. Therefore my heart is glad. All mercy of the Lord is on them that keep his covenant, and remembering His voice, do keep His commandments. Whoso is wise and will observe these things, will understand the loving-kindness of the Lord.

I am going to use a word I shall not use again to you. That word is handicapped—a word little understood.

The only man who is really blind is the man who cannot see, all about him, the opportunity to serve his God. Such a man, though he may have perfect physical vision, is still walking in spiritual darkness.

The only man who is unable really to walk, is the man who refuses to walk with God. Such a man, though he may have perfect physical locomotion adopts the gait of the Devil, if he moves forward in hardness of heart.

The only man who is really paralyzed, is the man who does not feel another's need. Such a man, though he may have full control of all his physical faculties, is insensible to concern and true sympathy and his only reflexes are those of his own selfish intent.

The only man who is really maimed is the man who has, himself, amputated from his life and practice all decency and honor. Such a man, though he may possess all his bodily members, is without the essential invisible additions of brotherhood which justify his existence.

The only man who is really deaf is the man who does not heed God's word. Such a man, though the organism of his ears may be perfect, does not hear because he will not listen.

Regarding handicaps, I, myself, was born with the most embarrassing and the only fun-poking one of all, the affliction of severe stammering. When I was a child, it was mental anguish for me to be obliged to speak to anyone, and when I was called upon to answer in the classroom, I often wished that I could die. No span of life is so fertile, for the planting of faith, as is childhood. In Bible history I had learned about Moses, who also stammered. When God directed him to give to the people of Israel, His, God's laws, God recognized Moses' dilemma. He sent to Moses an eloquent orator, Aaron, and Aaron was a cripple. Thus God selected to direct and lead His chosen nation, two men who, though physically imperfect, were spiritually superior, because they possessed the strength of spirit and the fortitude of faith, to instill in those about them the only worthwhile and enduring thing there is. Namely, belief in God, and hope of everlasting life.

St. Paul was the greatest evangelist of all time, yet he was an epileptic. This affliction he refers to as "a thorn in the flesh." The flesh is of no importance to God. It will become dust. The heart, mind, and soul are the instruments of worship. St. Paul spent his entire life wrestling with an incur-

able bodily condition, but he was on fire with the knowledge of the love and forgiveness of God, and the redeeming grace of the Christ.

I was taught, I have always believed, and now I know that God helps all of us, if we will only put ourselves in His keeping. I depended on God, as a child, to send someone to help me. He did. It was a teacher. She allowed me to write my classroom answers. After school was over she spent hours, which extended into weeks and months, helping me to learn to relax my spasmodic throat muscles, and to space my syllables.

All of our needs are different, but all of our help is the same. That help is God. Believe in Him. Trust Him. Pray to Him.

God rules the universe by laws: biological, physical, material, mathematical, and scientific. But His spiritual law exceeds and transcends them all. It is the only law that will survive. It is the one, everlasting, and eternal law.

The law of the Spirit enables a blind man to see a throne of celestial and radiant light, and a future life of perpetual perfection.

The law of the Spirit enables a deaf man to hear the heart-beat of his brother.

The law of the Spirit enables a man without arms or legs to lift the Banner of God and to march forward in His ranks.

The law of the Spirit enables a man without speech to excel the eloquence of all words by the example of a godly life.

The law of the Spirit enables a paralyzed man to

feel the throb of Eternity, which is the pulse of God.

We make an extensive study of all other laws, in order that we may profit by this knowledge. We neglect the most *important* one of all. In this neglect we deprive ourselves of the greatest benefit in this life and the only benefit in the life to come.

This spiritual law is the word of God, which was made flesh and sent to dwell among us in the body and voice of Jesus. When we follow His teachings we can conquer our own sorrow and despair. This world is a testing ground for eternity. None of us escape the trials which render us either fit, or unfit, for everlasting life.

In the world there are many things we find unequal, but in the Pilgrimage of the Soul, which leads to the Kingdom of God, every man has an absolute, and equal chance. God is no respecter of persons. He plays no favorites, and He promises never to forsake us. No circumstances can ever take away our chance of Salvation. God is our Heavenly Father. He loves and understands us. He loves us because we are His children. He understands us because we are of His own making. He created us.

The benefits of God do not begin when life is done. They begin today, and they increase after death. Jesus tells us that He stands at the door and knocks, and if any man hears His voice and opens the door, He will come in and abide with him. That word "him" means just what Jesus said it did—"any man." The rich man, the poor man, banker and beggar, landowner and wanderer. The master of fine arts and the sweat-drenched man in

63

a ditch. In the sight of God, they are all the same.

Don't keep the Saviour standing there waiting and longing to help you. The door that separates us from Him is the lack of our own understanding of just how much He really loves us. Seek that understanding. Take a firm grip on the handle of prayer, and open the door. Let God come into your life. He wants to help you. Try Him. Give Him a chance.

BENEDICTION.

May God bless and keep you this day and forever more. Amen.